Mo,
Thanks for your support and I hope you enjoy it. Also, thanks for taking the picture for the cover!

My Poetic Truth

By
Jon Chambers

Truth will keep us connected in a world full of deception

Jon Chambers

©2012 Jon Chambers
ISBN number: 9781467511995
Cover Design by: Kelsey Davis & Melissa Taurisano
Printed in the United States of America

Table of Contents

Introduction

"A bird doesn't sing because it has an answer, it sings because it has a song" –Lou Holtz

There are numerous reasons as to why I have decided to release this book at this point in time. One reason is my attempt to reach individuals who happen to have similar stories or similar unjustifiable thoughts and emotions that rage within their psyche. There are many thoughts and emotions people endure that they may choose to contain within and suppress. They may do this because of the fear-based premise that these emotions are not deemed socially acceptable. On the contrary, some people often release these emotions that dwell deep inside of them, but they are simply dismissed by the public as psychotic, foolish, or even blasphemous. Since I am able to address many of these beliefs and inward feelings on this poetic platform, I'm hoping that other people will be able to connect with them to eventually accept the suppressed and denied parts of themselves. When I was finally able to find individuals who had ways of thinking that were similar to my own, I no longer suppressed these thoughts and I was able to be true to myself. Someone else can possibly benefit from my writings in the same way that I have benefited from others.

Another reason for me writing this book is to introduce new ways of thinking about issues. Everybody has a story, and everybody has their own personal viewpoint to add to society. Only you can tell your personal story from your perspective. Everybody has their own personal experiences that have helped them to develop a viewpoint and opinion on life. I believe that interpersonal conscious conversation is the key to enhancing and facilitating growth. Conscious conversation is the open-minded dialogue that allows you to hear a different viewpoint, but also allows you to share your viewpoint with others. In order for this to occur, the notion of right and wrong must be completely destroyed and both parties must approach the conversation with the intent of learning and sharing their truth. For this to be successful, you must know yourself. This sounds simple, but many people become so caught up in the person they attempt to be in order to please society that they forget about the core of who they really are. It is not my intent in this book to correct your incorrect notions of life. My intent is simply to offer my perspective of the world as I see it. My introverted personality often prohibits me from being able to express these ideas in a people to people fashion. As a result, it is much easier for me to have conscious conversation through my writings and poetry. This is simply my truth in the form of poetry.

At the end of the day, all forms of art can serve as a form of entertainment. This is my next reason for writing this book. When I first began to write poetry growing up, I wrote it in the form of rap music. I was 10 years old, so the intent of these writings wasn't to convey some profound perspective on life, but it was rather to simply entertain me and my cousins. Entertainment can exist in the form of connecting to a feeling, but can also exist in the creative exploration of feelings. This is often evident when we go to see a movie. When we saw Denzel Washington play a crooked cop in the movie *Training Day*, we didn't speculate to ourselves whether or not Denzel or the writer of the script had actually been a crooked cop. We simply connected with the character and the emotions that he endured as a form of entertainment. It is also very possible to make a personal connection with a piece of art that the artist thought was purely fictional and imaginative. It's all about personal perception. I have poems that represent emotions and thoughts that I may have not directly experienced first-hand, but have observed and wished to document. You may be entertained in a way that is completely contrary to my writing intentions. I deem this perfectly fine. I always hated analyzing poetry in middle school. I felt as though the teacher was always looking for the "right" interpretation of the poem. In my eyes, the interpretation was always limitless. What I got out of the poem could never be wrong. That is how I feel about my own poetry. Unless you directly ask me what a poem means to me specifically or what message I was attempting to convey, I will never correct somebody else's interpretation of my poetry. That would simply be depriving them of their reading and connecting experience.

Lastly, there is one final reason why I have decided to write this book. That reason is my love for words and my love for expressing myself via my poetry. I would be writing poetry regardless of whether or not I decided to make these writings public. It is my way of organizing scattered thoughts in my brain, as well as a form of therapy to silence the voices that persist within my head. I think the quote at the beginning of the introduction embodies my reason for writing poetry. I'm not writing in an attempt to answer all of the questions of life. I'm not writing in an attempt to force my viewpoints of life onto my readers. I'm not writing in an attempt to spark some social movement or revolution. I simply write because I feel I have things to say. I feel that I have a song.

This book is very informal. These are my words directly and not the jargon of a professional editor. The punctuation and wording may not be ideal or up to the standards of what some may deem as proper grammar. Even the poems themselves are very informal. I don't follow any proper format when writing my poetry and I only use punctuation where I deem necessary. I use ellipses a lot in my poetry, which don't seem to be as prevalent in other poems. I don't believe that poetry, or even writing in general has to follow a specific format. I am content with my writing as long as it comes across in the way I mean it to, and as long as it flows easily to the reader regardless of how it is structured. Anyways... I'm done rambling. Welcome to my poetic truth, and I hope you can take something from it.

Words

Limiting language suffocates my spirit
It serves my soul no justice
It saddens my expressive potential
Its purpose can never fully manifest

There aren't enough words to describe these vibrations
To accurately express this universal rhythmic pulse
To correctly guide us through this three dimensional prism
To properly perceive emotional passion

Limiting language... our current stage in evolution
Representing our inability to communicate complex concepts
Representing our conscious interpretation of unconscious realities
Give me the words that comprehensively depict my truth

The Painter's Plight

"In a decaying society, art, if it is truthful, must also reflect decay. And unless it wants to break faith with its social function, art must show the world as changeable, and help to change it" –Ernst Fischer

The Austrian writer Ernst Fischer scribed these words that struck a chord in me that was deep-rooted somewhere in the midst of my judgments and ignorance. For a period time, I had been submitting to the close-minded and self-rejecting thinking that says all art should be positive and uplifting. I believed that anything depicting negativity was irresponsibly condoning it. Somewhere along my journey, I came to the realization that this couldn't be further from the truth. Regardless of the morality, art provides a platform for universal emotional clearing, and brings you a sense of oneness with the world if you are open to its reality. Art can also serve as news, by making the masses knowledgeable of the trials and triumphs of un-traveled terrain.

Art has existed for years in many different and often times contradictory places. Art is more than a painting that depicts a comfortable and idealistic illustration of society. It is that and so much more. It is music, movies, agriculture, architecture, graffiti, poetry, prose, photography, fashion, comedy, gaming, graphic design, etc. I've come to the conclusion that everything is art. Life is art. Everything from a beautiful sunset to the starving bum on the park bench is art. The only thing that a different and exclusive form of artwork will do is pinpoint a particular emotion or a particular creative depiction of life through the artist's unrestricting mind. So in a society where decay is not by any means extinguished, it is almost essential that art reflects this same decay that Fischer has alluded to.

This first collection of poems is me grappling with this concept. "Tears of Sad Clowns" dives into an acceptance of undesired emotions through artistic expression. It visually depicts the tears of the clown running its makeup into the street to create an "abstract masterpiece." Everything has beauty through divine eyes. Therefore, beauty cannot be confined to what may resonate with a particular culture or individual. It also cannot be confined to the imaginary good that contrasts the imaginary "bad" or "evil" that our minds have needlessly constructed. There is beautiful art in the tears of seemingly permanently happy clowns, which is simply a metaphor for our society.

The section comes to a close with "The Rhythm." This piece questions the validity of searching for truth by simply submitting to another individual's truth. In the end, it concludes that such searches are only counterproductive, and that becoming one with your own truth is the only accurate truth. Dancing to the rhythm of your own drum in this sense doesn't mean egotistically and arrogantly being close-minded to another's viewpoint. It simply means becoming one with your experiences and emotions while accepting them as yours instead of attempting to mask them. Let the plight of the painter reflect the decay of the world; but let's not forget the second part of Fischer's quote. Art must also show the world as changeable, and not simply be a concrete fixated view of your truth as one that should necessarily be adopted by all. Art will naturally help change the world through the wisdom and emotional connections brought to light by the artist.

Tour of My Mind

Enter into the gates of serenity and peace
The table where solitude and tranquility shall feast
The mask uncovered... the untold truth
The faucet of bliss... the fountain of youth
Travel first through right side of my mind
Where the music shrine puts me in tune with the divine
Travel through the right side of my brain
The one with true emotion... the suffering and shame
Travel next through the left side of my mind
And observe its ever most intricate design
Where the logic defies a concealed emotion
And reality destroys the creative devotion
Once you can navigate through my fear and doubts
And tear up the roots where ignorance sprouts
My mind will surpass the realms hate
My mind uncovers the place my future awaits

The Painter's Plight

Emotions in my heart hide behind words
The voices in my head linger in limbo
Lowering the bars in this prison
Give me a canvas to depict these dark tales
Give me a gun that shoots starts to light up the world

Awaiting the new earth and heaven after the holy war
Diminishing dangerous distinctions
Oneness appears beyond the veil
Awaiting future hopes that the present harbors

I write this prose for angelic con-artists
Hoping the world sees the light through your darkness

Tears of Sad Clowns

Tears of sad clowns flood Wall Street
Their makeup paints an abstract masterpiece
Mother earth becomes sorrow's salvation
Representing a mask-free moment of emotion
Painting the blood of the cold hearts
The hearts shatter like glass to the tempo of jazz
Painting the pride of the compassionate
The heads lie dormant on a Petri dish

The colors of the portrait mix together turning white
Only comprehensible with knowledge of darkness
The colors imitate the visible spectrum
The patterns imitate the constructed cosmos

Infinite artists on this canvas called life
Creating immeasurable realities
Defeating the imaginary idealism
Accepting the tears of the clown
The tears that drown…
Suffocating the body, rejecting ourselves

My Paintbrush

With an empty easel... my paintbrush tells it all
For it will never judge me... when I stumble and fall
That which is not painted... to be marketed or sold
But that which is painted... to tell the untold
With each and every stroke... the truth is revealed
Where nothing is subject to how the world may feel
My paintbrush does not fabricate... it does not lie
The works live on... it does not die
I am an artist... not a business man
For the path to the monetary is sinking sand
Temporary satisfaction is a devious plan
Maybe one day the world will understand
My paintbrush paints you a picture so vivid
The thick bold strokes are still oh so timid
That which is not painted... to be marketed or sold
But that which is painted... to tell the untold

The Rhythm

Book after book… page after page…
Act after act… stage after stage…
Calling it freedom… still trapped in a cage…
Was I finding myself… or was I fooling myself?

Teachers wanna teach me… but their words don't reach me
Preachers wanna tell me what I'm doing is wrong…
The givers of the knowledge are attorneys in disguise…
So if I don't be the judge… I'll be greeting my demise

There seems to be fewer giants…
Their shadows so crowded…
Their shoulders so heavy…

The doctrine that is taught couldn't be more sound
But a doctrine is just words… verbs and nouns
If you follow every word that is written in a text…
You'll never know success
He'll remain a distant relative… causing you distress
Disguised as an angel, seeking pleasures of the flesh
I thought I had a date with destiny…
But it was a demon in a dress

From now on I think I'll follow my own wisdom
But how do you make that decision?
How do you decipher between a veil and a vision?
When you hear your own drum… just dance to the rhythm

Religious Inquiry

"I believe in Christianity as I believe that the sun has risen: not only because I see it, but because by it I see everything else" -C.S. Lewis

We as humans are a complex species. We have been given this intellectual ability to wonder about things, draw conclusions, and ultimately the capacity to deal with issues of morality. The human brain is a gift and a curse. It gives us the capacity to solve problems and build skyscrapers, but it can also create problems that are nonexistent and bring us out of touch with our feelings and intuitive guidance. For lifetimes, humans have used this intellect to draw conclusions about the meaning of life and have created numerous religions and ideologies that directly reflected the times of their existence.

I was raised as a Christian, under the Baptist denomination. There was never a question as to whether or not I was to attend church on Sunday morning. When that's all you know, it is hard to have a differing opinion. I'm almost certain that my religious inquiry began in the second grade. I had a friend by the name of Dan who was Jewish, and I was so intrigued to discover that there were religious people out there who didn't practice Christianity and believe that Jesus Christ was the messiah. I started seeing religion as hereditary.

Ever since then I've always questioned religion. Not just my religion, but religion as a whole. Who knows why? Maybe it was my INTP personality profile according to the Myers Briggs test. Maybe it was astrological; the fact that Pisces aligned with Mars on May first when I was born. Regardless of the reason, there was no way I would dare speak out. Even when I did, my questions and analytical observations were swiftly greeted with contradictory bible passages that were the alleged ultimate truth. So I wrote off my questions for years and just regarded my anti-biblical observations as the devil testing my faith. I considered myself crazy for even thinking anything opposite of what I was being told. So I conformed.

Unfortunately, outward conformity did very little to bring

the voices inside of my head to a standstill. Poetry became my outlet to release these voices in an effort to gain back my sanity. After researching numerous religions to educate myself, I began to realize that the numerous religions across the world all seemed to have more in common than they had differences. They all seemed to be deep-rooted in metaphysical experiences that connect you to the divine source. The differences were based on technicalities, traditions, the unverifiable phenomena of how the world will come to an end, and what occurs after life on this earth plane. I believe that the divine connection is real. I believe that we are all here for reasons that our three dimensional bodies that perceive five senses cannot comprehend. I also believe that the divine connection is within us, just as it was with Jesus Christ. In addition, I believe that this connection to divinity is possible regardless of the limiting language you use to describe it, regardless of the ideology you choose to follow, and regardless of whether you choose to follow a structured institutional ideology at all. Words and language just simply represent our attempts as humans to communicate concepts that are sometimes beyond normal sensory comprehension. Many religions just use different language to describe phenomena that even scientists can't deny.

One of my favorite philosophers is Alan Watts. He spoke of religion in terms of a metaphor that I believe explained it perfectly. He said that religion is like a finger that is pointing at the moon. The problem then occurs when we mistake the finger for the actual moon itself. When we forget what we were searching for and get too hung up on rituals and mandates that humans have created to make sense of it all. He goes on to say that what religion points at is something that is not religious at all. This was a very interesting viewpoint on the nature of religion that made me assess religion in a different way.

Pieces like "The Cross" and "Angel" are examples of me embracing my Christianity upbringing, which I continue to do to this day. Denying Christianity would be denying a part of me and a part of the history of my existence that played a key role in shaping my current beliefs. I accept it. While accepting it, I view complaints and grievances as simply my inner mind projecting suppressed beliefs that I harbor within and have chosen to ignore.

That still doesn't stop me from expressing these thoughts I harbor. "The Crazy Man" explores the concept that Jesus could return in the form of anybody. In the poem, I depict a crazy homeless man that I decline to provide monetary aid to. It turns out that the man I called crazy was Jesus Christ himself. The poem "Morality" discusses philosopher Friedrich Nietzsche's views on how morality and religion was crafted over the years. The practicality behind these ideas drove me to consider his philosophy. It's interesting that many organizations around the world and throughout history allege to take their moral views from the Bible, though so many different and contradictory moral standards have been implemented all from this same source. It's almost as if we construct our own morality, and simply find scriptures and text to defend ourselves. "A Selfish Paradise" is merely me exploring the selfish egotistic way heaven is often described in sermons. "Root of Evil" is an exploration of the relationship between money, God, and evil.

While some of my views and perceptions may seem to contradict one another on the surface, I'm simply being honest to the complex ever-changing truths that my mind endures. Hopefully we can all continue to give the world our truths in an effort to evolve and come to grips with the ultimate truth. I do not write to convince you of my views or to debate yours; I write so that my views are on the table and so that we can collectively grow together and embrace each other's differences. I don't have the answers. Socrates once said that a wise man knows that he knows nothing at all. Today's truths often turn out to be tomorrow's folklore. That being said, I'll simply stay true to what I believe, live in the moment, remain conscious of inquiry, and speak my open-minded truths to actively participate in humanity's conscious evolution.

The Cross

Nobody understands me… nobody but God
This is why I am struck by the enemy's rod
The blood… the sweat… the tears… the pain
But I trust you father… for I know it is not in vain
Nothing will occur that will defy your will
Even my wished upon fate… even the blood spilled
For all who have sinned… for all those lost
It is for your everlasting life… that I carry the cross
Father forgive them… though all they can do is laugh
Father forgive them… though I know you already have
For they know not the sins they have committed against you
They don't discern me as the savior… nor believe my word is true
Why have you forsaken me… why have you left?
But you never truly did… my spirit you would protect
For all who sin… for all who are lost
You may seek everlasting life… because I carried the cross

Angel

A touch from the rear that remains unseen
Existent in ever mother, ever child, every fiend
Blind eyes never depict what lies behind
So mute but so dynamic... so marvelous, so divine
Captivating souls in a deceptive disguise
But deception is warranted, so our souls can survive
They thrive for knowledge, but the wisdom shaped the trace
We unconsciously follow it... partaking in fate
Too often the gratitude remains absent in return
But the touch still returns when the fire burns
The fire that can strip you of your aspirations
The fire that blinds eyes... demonic damnation
Until the heavenly waters rain down to diminish
Until the blaze ceases to exist and is finished
So much pain... suffering and strife
Thank God I had an angel in my life

The Crazy Man

We laugh… dismiss… spit in his face
The trash heap is where he gathers his dinner plate
The concrete ground is where he rests his head
Nobody listens… they condemn instead
Nobody listens… it's as if he was dead
Nobody attends to the blood that is shed
Holding the remedy… we refuse to approach the manger
Our pride just never lets us feel for a stranger
So we pass him by… we're too sane to converse
Not realizing we are the ones plagued by the curse
We pass him by… clutching our purse
Not grasping his magnitude… grasping his worth
One day he approached me… soliciting aid
I abruptly declined… as if I was afraid
I watched him ascend… recognizing it was He
I was left behind… the crazy one was me

A Selfish Paradise

He refuses to covet his neighbor's possessions
Caring and giving has become his obsession
He appears to be headed in the right direction
He just wants to make it to paradise…

He won't be belittled by Satan's wrath
He won't be corrupted by the powers of cash
He appears to be traveling along the right path
He just wants to make it to paradise…

A paradise… full of self-interest and greed
A paradise of golden roads for the ones who deceive
A paradise… full of wrongdoers who chose to "repent"
A paradise… full of bad karma from corrupt intent

A selfish paradise is hard to sell…
So it's sold with fear… "We need to escape hell"
The paradise they preach isn't paradise to me
Just self-consumption… hidden behind religious beliefs

Morality

Maybe morality was created to disarm the master
The master of external exploitation to empower
Darwin's minions praising the fourteenth King Louis
Personifying the psyche of Health Ledger's last role

Maybe morality was created to arm the slave
The hopeless and oppressed… desiring their grave
God's creators praising fables of moral truth
Personifying the psyche of the subjugated Egyptians
Creating laws from the fiction… deceptive diction
Misdirected visions… religion…

Power… survival… the undeniable motivations
The masters get their power by constructing corporations
While the meek get their power through immoral accusations
Making declarations to promote it to the congregation

Maybe morality itself is immoral
Voices of the gods given breath by the mortals

Commercialized Christ

Born of a virgin... son of Saint Nick
Wrapped in green and red... Joseph's coat of many colors
When it rained deer, green trees would sprout
Money trees with bloody leaves
Set ablaze with multiple flames

Born on the North Pole... greeted by three elves
They gave gifts of cookies, milk, and a red suit
They carried him through town on a one horse open sleigh
His birth would coincide with the solstice

This was scribed with creative hands
Just like the Holy word... scribed by man
On an unmarked day... these things were written
A commercialized Christ... for commercialized Christians

Church Clothes

Why should I change my appearance for God to talk to me?
I know that's not how it's said... but it's how it came across to me
The more clothes you wear... the more you seem lost to me
Thinking heaven's your destination... but you lost the key
It's one thing to show respect in God's presence
But it's another thing when appearance makes you lose the essence
As if outside of the church that very God wasn't present
Do I need these gold ceilings just to hear the message?
If you gave up one's self... to a being that is higher
Time wouldn't allow you to assess your neighbor's attire
Conforming to an image... because "that's just how it is"
But they know not what they do... please Lord forgive
God can't see the façade we put up for our peers
All He sees is the soul... how it truly appears
In order to receive Him... and be made whole
Don't dress up your body... just submit your soul
We forgot why we were here... because of these extravagant
clothes
The devil snuck in the back door... and received control
Whether you dress like a thug... or dress like a reverend
You won't be wearing anything on judgment day... at the gates of
heaven

Root of Evil

Faith of mustard seeds sprouting roots to all evil
Growing forbidden fruit on the tree of life
Forbidden fruit and empty stomachs
Grapes fermented into wine and drunken obese bourgeoisie

Numerous naive neo-Eves
Greeted by sly serpents promising knowledge and wisdom
Ashamed by the naked truth
False egos override blissful ignorance

Faith of mustard seeds sprouting roots to all evil
Growing healthy green leaves with president faces
One tenth of what you garner belongs to the divine
At least that's how it's written...

I guess even God is 10% wicked

The Hands of Man

The fires of Hell...
Sparked by a match made in heaven
Burning bridges to the Promised Land
Drowning the sheep...

The fires of Hell...
Sparked by a muse strumming tunes
The son of the early dawn casting darkness
Molded by the hands of man

The gates of Heaven...
Open to the righteous children of Israel
Closed to those disowning the Christ
An incentive unknown to the living

The gates of Heaven...
The dwelling place of the almighty
The place where his servants submit
Molded by the hands of man

The hands of man...
Filling in the gaps of what they don't understand

Philosophical Phases

How did we get here?
What are we doing?
Placed in this three dimensional prism
Here with no sensory guidance that's not tainted
Here in the microcosm of a galaxy
Here with these minds to think and philosophize fallacies

Where are the limits?
Where does this evolution finish?
When does everything become clear?

These questions are at war with people with answers
But their answers don't seem to bring me peace
They give me more speculations…
I need to silence these voices… I need more meditation

Wars in my mind… constant debates
Are we divine destiny or dead weight?
Did man evolve or did God create?
In the end I have no answers…
Just a head the aches

Mind Control

"Any writer, I suppose, feels that the world into which he was born is nothing less than a conspiracy against the cultivation of his talent" –James A. Baldwin

I reached a point in my life where I didn't know what to believe in anymore. I began to question everything I had been told by every teacher, parent, elder, policeman, politician, etc. This strong skepticism about everything made me want to pick everything apart. It made me want to find flaws in everything I had once taken for granted as absolute certainty. I stopped paying attention to politics; I thought it was all lies. I stopped watching the news; I thought it was all propaganda. I stopped believing history; I thought it was all tainted. Not saying that any of these statements are entirely false, but my mind was so made up that these were no longer solely possibilities. They were rather cut and dry realities that the rest of society was blinding themselves to. This train of thinking would eventually make me very susceptible to conspiracy theorists. A vicious cycle of never-ending doubt would soon ensue.

I'm honestly unsure as to what took my skepticisms about everything over the top. Maybe I read George Orwell's *1984* one too many times. Maybe I gave *Zeitgeist* one too many views on YouTube. Maybe I gave Alex Jones' website one too many visits. Whatever the case may be, I was hooked. I started to realize that everything known to man had some form of conspiracy behind it. Somebody susceptible to things of this nature will begin to believe that there really IS a hidden agenda behind everything. It got to the point where I was even questioning some of my favorite hip-hop artists, believing that some of them were actually devil worshiping soldiers for a larger corporate agenda.

I now realize why this was a never ending cycle that would never reach closure without some sort of effort on my own part. I was now falling victim to the very thing I attempted to condemn. I was no longer looking for facts. I was looking for a good story. What I should've been doing was attacking and questioning the conspiracy theorists with the same fervor that I attacked the politician and the corporations. I was attacking blind evidence-free absolute truth with more blind evidence-free absolute truth. The whole time I was fighting against mind control, while sitting in front of these conspiracy theorists and letting them program my thinking to fit their preposterous proposals. I still pay attention to conspiracies and recognize the possibility of certain things being one way or the other, but I don't let them control my opinion as I did in the past.

The poem "Dr. Demon" is about the pharmaceutical industry. It has always been my belief that pharmaceutical companies were nothing but glorified drug dealers that happen to have governmental support. The poem is an attempt to personify my vitriol with words. In "For Years to Come" I discuss this mind control in the context of an enemy to mankind that's spiraling out of control with no end in sight. In "Sinister Suits" I try to tap into the demon that I see ever so present underneath the suits and smiles of businessmen.

It's very strenuous viewing the world through the biased lens of constantly being on the receiving end of dishonesty and deception. Seeing how I am an introvert who lives in my head the majority of the day, the soldiers at the entry gate to my mind go into stage 5 terrorism alert when they believe an enemy is either approaching or has already breached security. These are the nihilistic tales of a troubled mind refusing to program to the same frequency as the ignorant blinded masses. Little did I know that I was in control of my mind the entire time. I was simply pointing to the outside world looking for someone to blame. I thought everything and everybody was trying to change me into something I wasn't. This was maybe because I didn't know who I truly was to begin with. I was looking for acceptance and verification for my inward beliefs, when in actuality I hadn't yet even accepted them within myself. I began to see my pure artistic self-expression unappreciated and ignored. The natural defense mechanism is to perceive it as a conspiracy against my creativity and individuality. It was time for a revolution.

Control

I fight the forces that force feed
I fight the forces until I'm freed
Even if they're telling me the right way to proceed
I fight the forces until I'm freed

Even if I'm obedient to these forces
I'll perform angelic actions with wrong motives
Fearful of my dictator's judgment
Troubled presents and future fears

I can't submit...
I can't be the dummy for you ventriloquists
I can't give you control
I can't be on stage with strings tied to my soul

You call it stubborn... I call it liberation
You call it close-minded... I call it elevation
I fight the forces that force feed
I fight the forces until I'm freed

I'm just doing my sanity a deed...
I hope I succeed

Dr. Demon

Prescribing poison for profit... commercialized drugs
Televised villains... commercialized thugs
Paying off doctors... devils with degrees
Speaking false tongue towards diminishing disease
Prescribing pills for the ills... sickening side-affects
On the road to well-being you collide with death
Stalin with a stethoscope... a civilized savage
Madness...

Beautiful Backbones

Beautiful backbones, destroyed and dismantled
Put into submission to silence the sheep
Quiet the meek... let their voice-boxes shatter...
Like the opposite of the box that holds their minds hostage
The rectangular frame used to program their brains
Lucrative lies of love so the romance remains
Deceptive kisses turn tongues to bullets
Exiting cold hard lips of misused knowledge
The blood spills out...
The love spills out...
Misdirection and propaganda cover the wounds
From mothers' wombs to lovers' tombs
Making life a widow...
But that female dog will soon find another groom

Sinister Suits

Vulchers in lamb's wool speaking foreign tongue
Jargon that resembles hieroglyphics to the common man
Powerful maneuvers masqueraded with a smile
Murderous minds masqueraded by the naïve hair groomer
Staring at one another's ties, praying for their demise
Wishing to take the tie and suffocate the savage until he's silenced
Turn it into a noose and let his shined shoes dangle
Then decapitate his demonic mind and send it to a cannibal

These are the hidden memoirs of a sinner in a suit
Heart cold as the winter, eating dinner with his youth
And when his seed is of the age to wear a suit of his own
He plans to gives his family closet more skeleton bones

For Years to Come

Fixated on this broken pedestal,
The faces blindly follow.
Corrupted with the power,
My heart beating so hollow.

They mistake my falsehoods for truth
They mistake my masquerade for compassion
They mistake my deception for perfection
They mistake my materials for progression

I am the law...
I am the truth...
I am the lie that corrupts the youth...

In my hands I can create...
In my hands I can devour...
No one man should have all of that power

They've created nations on my lies...
Continued the tradition even after my demise...
Intellectual thought is greeted with a gun...
Blinding the truth... for years to come

Potential

Society is blinding... to the ways of the mind
The untapped potential behind the blinds
The five blinds... that we call the ultimate truth
Where authority would discourage the curious youth
In a world where war is the answer... and religion divides
Their questions unanswered... their dreams denied
Creativity is shunned... so they're given a disguise
Never will their body and their spirit align
Brought up to conform... brought up under a veil
Brought up to masquerade... brought up to fail
So instead of awakening to our divine light
We simply blend in... like chameleons in the night
Surrounded by pitch black... holding a pitchfork
Murdering our minds... showing no remorse

Schoolyard Murder

Quick to assign problems... but skim past the message
Quick to teach self-interest... but skim past the ethics
Quick to tell us our history... but skim past the truth
The original man came from Africa... they skim past the roots
European explorations... but they skim past the rape
The slavery and murders while they smiled in their face
Thanksgiving? I don't wish to celebrate deception
Falling victim to a hoax used for misdirection
Conformity and greed... disguised as education
This is a corporate run land that's disguised as a nation

School gives you a good job...
If you pay the cost to get through it
Then you become a slave...
Just like that professor who 'taught' you how to do it

Ever since K-5... our freethinking was lost
They took the wood from our pencils and made it into a cross
They told us we need money... never-mind a hobby
They took the chalk from the chalk board... and sketched our
bodies

Stunted Potential

Every day we get further from our youth
And every day we get further from the truth
Creative minds, silenced by ill-advised science
Creative hands, threatened by a list of demands
We strip them of their paintbrush... take away their tools
We strip them of experience... place them in a school
Another victim of conformity... another educated fool
Another free thinker... falling victim to the rules
Another great artist... told not to create
Another seeker of love... programmed to hate
Your parents are programmed... so nobody can warn you
That the schools don't educate... they just conform you
The mind is turned off... questions unanswered
Televisions turned on... visual cancer
Another robot... to be appointed king
So he can pass the tradition off to his offspring

Society is a Black Hole

Society appears to be a big black hole
When one becomes enLIGHTened… the truth is untold
It silences our heart… destroys our soul
Committing our spirit… we lose control
Darkness is simply the absence of light
Death is simply the absence of life
In a black hole… the light can't escape
We are pulled by this force… to await our fate
My whole life has been plagued by this inevitable end
So I dwell in my own mind… my very best friend
My whole life is a big circle of society's lies
It will eventually lead to my free will's demise
Society appears to be a big black hole
When one becomes enLIGHTened… the truth is untold
I wish to become enLIGHTened… and let my light show
But the light becomes trapped… so the world would never know

Revolutionary Channeling

"The most radical revolutionary will become a conservative the day after the revolution" –Hannah Arendt

My obsession with being controlled by society began to spiral out of control. In my mind, being controlled was no longer a fear. It was a reality. It was a reality that was destructive and needed to be abolished. It was a reality that I needed to fight against and expose to the masses. I admired people that were able to speak out against the system, regardless of whether or not they were speaking factual evidence from a completely honest place. Revolutionists throughout history were my greatest source of inspiration throughout this time. In addition, documents like the *Communist Manifesto* provided the framework for my perception on what a revolution should be and why it was necessary. One of my favorite rock bands is Coldplay. In their song entitled "A Rush of Blood to the Head" they include the lyrics: "So I'm going to buy a gun and start a war, if you can tell me something worth fighting for." These lyrics embodied my state of mind at this point of time in my life. The only problem was the last part of the quoted lyrics. I didn't have enough information on anything that I despised to have anything worth fighting for. The irrational revolutionary channeling had begun.

I began to believe that revolutions had to be bloody to have a sincere effect on the oppressor. As a result, I also believed that the only real revolutionaries were martyrs who had given their life for their cause. Even though being willing to die for your beliefs has its validity, the martyr attitude I had adopted became troublesome. This viewpoint was altered when I read a book by Gary Zukav entitled *Seat of the Soul*. Here is an excerpt from this life-changing book:

"Individuals who experience what might be thought of as a martyr attitude see themselves as giving all that they have to others. They see this as a form of loving, but in truth the love that they give is contaminated because it is so filled with sorrow for themselves. A

45

sense of guilt and powerlessness clouds the energy from their hearts and so when their affection is felt by another it does not feel good, actually. It feels somehow thick with need, yet the need is never articulated, so their love feels like cement pulling you."

I'm not saying that you should believe everything you read, because of course that's what got me stuck in the middle of this revolutionary channeling in the first place. What I'm saying is that I read this excerpt and it resonated someplace true within my heart. I felt the sorrow for myself that Zukav explains, as well as the sense of guilt and powerlessness. This realization eventually led me to do some reflecting on myself and my motives, but we'll save that for the next chapter.

Another troublesome aspect of my attitude was anger, which I believe was simply a form of fear. It was a deep-rooted fear of being controlled beyond my ability alter. Revolutions can't be conducted out of fear, but they must rather be conducted through love. When revolutions are done out of fear, you are simply attempting to change others so that you feel more secure. When revolutions are done out of love there isn't any forcing, but rather a conscious violence-free petition to give voice to an idea that may have been silenced or ignored. It is also an idea that is not selfish and biased, but rather an idea that is conscious of its effects on human evolution as well as intimate empathetic human interaction.

This section begins with a piece entitled "Fear of Rebellion." It poetically describes an issue known as the free rider problem. The free rider problem states that in an enormous group, individual contributions are very small and difficult to monitor. That being the case, the completely rational individual will understand that his contribution makes very little difference to the whole and nobody would probably even notice if he/she contributes. The problem is when everybody has this same state of mind and everybody succumbs to the fear of being the odd one out. This poem addresses the problem and urges for collective action. Ironically, me writing this poem without any action of my own places me right in the middle of this issue. I'm placed right in the middle of the individuals soliciting change without enough courage to take the first step themselves. "The Pledge" is simply my rendition of the Pledge of Allegiance. I simply deemed this version more appropriate and accurate to my views on America and justice at this point in my life. The section comes to a close with a piece entitled "In the End." In this piece I simply explain the detachment I felt from the rest of society. This was before I realized everything I saw in society was merely a reflection of me. This was long before I began to experience oneness.

Fear of Rebellion

Why are we afraid to situate and take a stand?
Maybe we just fear what we don't understand
Do we realize that we build their homes?
Wash their feet as they sit on their throne?
Without compliance… they cease to exist
They reign supreme when we refuse to resist
They don't educate us… so we think we're trapped
So to this close-minded state of mind… we adapt
We wonder if everything we have worked for will vanish
If everything we control… will we no longer manage
Who would rebel against their own protection?
The path in this logic is a fool's direction
The neglectors are outnumbered by the ones they neglect
The suppressors are outnumbered by the ones they suppress
They are the ones afraid… so they propagandize doubt
They realize we are the ones they can't survive without

Faux Pas

Yield not to the ways of man
Learn to rebel... learn to take a stand
Yield not to the ways of tradition
Learn to provoke change... learn to make a difference
Question authority... until the truth is told
Stay away from the grass that glitters with gold
Wear not the garments of the accepted regime
They are masking insecurities... nothing is how it seems
Read their books with a curious mind
Unless you use your own eyes... to the truth you are blind
Re-examine their politicians... and see how they deceive
As the world follows the mold... and lets them lead
Reject the ways of this planet that is third from the sun
Reject it... because of the blind misleader it has become
Yield not to the ways of man
Learn to rebel... learn to take a stand

The Martyr

Nothing is real in this world of hate
Preaching my views… awaiting my fate
Nothing is real in this world of lies
Making them rebel… awaiting my demise
No I won't conform… no you can't oblige
I will not live in this world… drunk with its wine
I will not live in this world… if love is masked
When they kill my body… my soul shall rest at last
Take my body… free my soul
Make me complete… make me whole
Standing up for ones rights… the cardinal sin
Standing up… just to tell how you feel within
But you can't challenge the views… of those who rule
The ones with artillery… those ignorant fools
Goodbye cold world… maybe one day you'll see
What the world really needs… is more people like me

When I'm Gone

It's a shame I was so misunderstood
Not afraid to do what another man should
Anti-social... trusting not even my reflection
Maybe that explains my depression
Maybe that explains my social regression
If you hear from me... you're simply an exception
At least my soul will reunite with God
Destiny fulfilled... I have completed my job
This earth no longer needs my shell
So take what I've written... the world you shall tell
I knew soon they'd love me... I knew soon they'd care
Now looking at my casket... all they can do is stare
When will this good karma finally collide with me?
I know that it's coming... but I don't think I'll be alive to see
When I'm gone... just know everything is destined to be
And I've completed the path that was destined for me

Heterodoxy

Conformists to my culture may view me as a rebel
Religious advocates may view me as a devil
The politicians say I lack love for the nation
But I'm a slave studying ways of 18th century Haitians
Minds designed Satan making minds complacent
Let minds defy hatred and align constellations
I bet it coincides with divine elevation
And cracks seals scribed in the lines of Revelations

Liberated options led to the despising of the doctrines
Self-interpretation and dividing was adopted
The greatest minds succeeded in making history re-write
While lesser minds feared and conspired against the Christ
In orthodox circles what we preach is a pollution
Passing for a prophet will result in persecution
What you call heresy is often the solution
So think before you try to crucify the revolution

Lady Liberty

She's frozen in time... peers with still eyes
Facing the land of promise... watching its demise
Enslaving under freedoms name... resembling a steeple
Closed books... closed minds... dismembering its people
She's never been faithful... she'll forever be a harlot
She stood still and watched... as New York turned scarlet
It's evident she had knowledge of the planes
A grand scheme to ensure the black gold was obtained
She doesn't wish to see us educated and humane
She'd rather see us high on cocaine...
Drunk off champagne... poisoning our brain
While her Uncle Sam uses you to prolong her reign
Heartless... she never sheds tears into the stream
She's a swindler standing on the Hudson selling dreams
Her heart's cold... and her flesh is made of stone
Peering with still eyes at the place we call home

The Heist

Manipulation is the greatest of their weapons
No armor surrounds them... for we are their protection
Their infantry is us... we are their soldiers
They say in God they trust... but give him the cold shoulder
They reign supreme at the place we call home
Gave us a promise that we would never be alone
Arouse fear in our hearts by constructing an attack
An attack on our own soil... that concealed the facts
You would think we would have opened up a history book
To that times of that Nazi... and the way things looked
The way he seduced the people with his words
In the midst of the blind... an overtaking occurred
The heist has begun... begun once again
To corrupt the masses... and steal the souls of its men
The heist is here... America has attacked
Let's see if you are one of the few... who can keep their soul in tact

The Pledge

I pledge allegiance
To the lies
Of the divided states if America

And to the republic
With the devil it shall dance
One nation... forgetting God

Division is visible
No liberty... no justice
Like Rome we shall fall

Horses with Blinders

Horses with our blinders on...
Dr. Experience grimaces with no students
Love is confined to designs architected by self
Hate is subconsciously breeding envy in your minds mansion
Crazed by a capsule addiction and demonic diction
Divided by conquerors and their poisoned prescriptions
These oxymorons put us in submission
Proper politician... Christ-like Christian

Horses with our blinders on...
Experience is a salesman with a pink slip
Creativity is lost in the left brain's numbers
Conformity is slowly breeding detrimental groupthink

Until the day we break these psychological chains,
We'll just be horses with our blinders on...
Living in vain

In the End

In the beginning was a man... followed by his n̵
In the beginning was a tree... whose fruit they a̵
Nothing to lose... but everything at stake
An ongoing cycle they would spark and create
In the beginning there was hope... for the human race
Until easily controlled to indulge and taste
For years we would conform... seeking higher terrain
Nothing will suffice... when there is more to gain
Why should I be held by the wages of accord?
That tell me in revenge I must seek my sword
Why should I limit the being I embody?
To an existence that is much more careless and shoddy
In the beginning was a man... followed by his mate
In the beginning was a tree... whose fruit they ate
In the end... I vow to rebel society's trees
Because in the end there's no society... all I have is me

Self-Reflection

"Everything that irritates us about others can lead us to an understanding of ourselves" –Carl Jung

I reached a stage in my life where I needed to reflect upon myself as opposed to casting judgment and blaming the world. This quote from Jung became increasingly relevant in my life when I began to see it manifest. Often times, it seems that we are most annoyed and disgruntled by outside situations that remind us of parts of ourselves that we have denied and suppressed. The reflection of ourselves that we project outward and manifest in other individuals can often be an unpleasant sight. I believe that at the core we are all connected. I've come to understand hating another individual as simply hating the suppressed potential within ourselves that would surface if we were given the same uncontrollable physiological makeup and environmental factors.

An easy example is the grade school bully. Most people are well aware that bullies often times turn out to be insecure and emotionally vulnerable. The reason is of unimportance, and could stem from a wide variety of environmental factors. The key here is that the bully often suppresses these insecurities and pretends as if they're nonexistent. Therefore, when the bully comes in contact with someone who appears insecure and vulnerable, he/she simply attacks. In essence they are attacking themselves. While attacking themselves they are also attempting to assure themselves that nothing about this fearful and defenseless nerd embodies anything they harbor within themselves. By doing this, they are simply suppressing their true feelings and emotions deeper and deeper instead of seeing themselves within their surroundings and using it as an opportunity to clear unattended emotions.

You project and perceive your reality. It's never the outside environment that causes your emotional reactions, but it's your views and perceptions of this reality you have projected that cause these reactions. At least that is how I've come to understand it. I read a book entitled *Emotional Clearing* by John Ruskan. This book really helped me identify suppressions and accept my emotions. It also helped me to articulate with words different revelations that I had come to understand without the ability to communicate them. I would recommend that book to anybody, regardless of how blissful, accepting, and worry free you pronounce yourself to be. We are all growing and evolving on this earth plane through the lessons and interactions of our surrounding environment. In essence, this surrounding environment is actually your inner reality projected onto the world. Deny the world, and you deny yourself.

This section starts off with a poem entitled "Running." I wrote this when I began to do some serious self-reflection. The basis is that I've been running from everything I see that I dislike, not realizing that I was only running from those qualities within myself. I have come to believe that unless you encounter your demons internally, you'll never escape them externally, because they were never external to begin with. "Shielded From Self" discusses the act of self-rejection. It reverts back to the premise that you cannot blame others for your feelings and the perception that you are creating about them. The section comes to a close with poems entitled "Demons" and "Exorcize Me." These poems simply state that the demons and devils that you often feel are attacking you are actually internal. I would highly recommend reflection and meditation upon the self in order to embrace and better understand your feelings. Just remember to embrace your feelings instead of using your mind to try to trick yourself into thinking that those feelings are illogical and not really existent.

Running

Divided by illusions... I'm forced into seclusion
I wish they understood that we live in a delusion
Maybe I wish they understand... mad at my own ignorance
Mad at my self-omitting conclusion
I sit dormant in my cave... pleading for evolution
I sit stagnant on destruction... pleading for a solution
I know the answers to every question they can ask
I know the pedestal's an illusion... but in its glory I bask
I tried to escape the corruption... escape the lies
So I departed to the lake... to pray to the skies
I tried to evade the conformists... avoid tradition
So I departed to the lake... to pursue something different
I wanted to pursue something true... something sacred
So I stripped my garments... and proceeded on naked
I left behind the profit... the evil self-motives
I left the mechanized cycle... to which I was devoted
But when I looked in the lake... all I could do was run
Because the reflection in the lake... was what I had been running
from

Perception

The masses are watching... their eyes wide open
Watching you mix and digest your potion
The same potion mixed by that serpent long ago
The one who slithered deception... and brought God's people
below
It's all perception... when prescribed with this prescription
It's all deception... which is why there's division
It's all for an act... it's all for an image
It's to be proactive... in order to disguise your blemish
Creativity is stunted... spiritual growth is forbidden
Because that only occurs when your ears don't listen
That only occurs when your third eye sees vivid
And your desire to control shall slowly diminish
Fitting into a group... shows harmony absent
And I love harmony... she buried control in a casket
Harmony doesn't seem to be concerned with perception
Or maybe that's just how she wants the story to read
Maybe that's just how she wants to be perceived

Green Grass

Bright green grass... Dying with the footsteps
Everything desired deemed demonic with hindsight
Signs glaring back with guidance ignored with ignorance
Everything I see is a reflection of my suppressions
Everything hated is a reflection of my denied self
Everything loved is my acceptance of what I harbor
Everything that's met without judgment is unfiltered
Everything that's observed with the ego is compared

Bright green grass... dying with the footsteps

Shielded From Self

Projected externally... creating unjust blame
Attempting to decipher the cause of the rain
The cause of the pain... suffering in vain
Thanks to repressed regrets and unconscious emotions
Contending with outside forces...
Contained by the invisible wall of the rebel's fortress
Extending the distance from the head to the heart

At war with energies divided by perception
Self-rejection... disguised as protection

Imaginary Identities

False realities created
Sacred realities of hatred
Blended with the love of the addict
Dependent to please illusory habits
Depicting distinctions dependently pleasing non-existent pleasure
Making it equivalent to pain... sun equivalent to rain...
The rain that creates roses equivalent to guns
Shooting bullets killing strangers equivalent to sons
Equivalent to none...
Zero is the solution to invisible sums
Sums of evil and good... crazy and sane
Educated and ignorant... heartless and humane
Dualistic potentials awaiting situations
Whether liberation, domination, or damnation
Provoked by temptation, starvation, and fixations
Infinite figments of imagination

Demons

Open the door... put your soul at ease
Don't taste the fruit... nor gaze at the trees
The power obtained is unmatched but deadly
Enclosed and imprisoned... but still set free
Open the door... dismiss your guard
For he is absent in the daylight... but awakes for the stars
So whenever his visibility is obsolete
Despite time of day... the soul is labeled deceased
Your closest companion could be the primary source
With compassion neglected... lacking remorse
Conquered by a force that reigns beyond control
Beyond the physical... in tune with the soul
Beyond what is seen... in tune with your thoughts
Beyond what you'll find... because your own being is lost
They dwell in the heathen... they dwell in the poisonous direction
But sometimes... they dwell in the mirror's reflection

Exorcize Me

I need the best religion
I need an exorcism

These forces disconnect me from myself
At least the self I thought I was
The self I told people I was

Who are you?
What have you done with me?
Or maybe you're a part of me...
The part I buried alive
You have risen to haunt me
You have risen to taunt me
Showing me who I really am

Helping my psychological see
This isn't possession...
This is just me

My Poetic Truth

Tales from the Dark Side

"There is no explanation for evil. It must be looked upon as a necessary part of the order of the universe. To ignore it is childish, to bewail it senseless" -W. Somerset Maugham

"Enlightenment is not imagining figures of light, but making the darkness conscious" -Carl Jung

After self-reflection, it was time to come to grips with the demons within. It was time to stop ignoring parts of myself that would simply manifest themselves in my environment and overtake my emotional stability. Everybody has thoughts within them that the civil and rational mind would consider evil and inhumane. Every single one of us has had doubts about our core belief system that may go against everything that we have been living for. Everybody has certain psychopathic urges that our "sanity" quickly dismisses and attempts to expunge. Why do you think we like violent movies so much? Why do you think we are so entertained by tyrants and heartless emotionless self-interested monsters? I would argue that this entertainment creates a metaphor for the battles going on within.

We all have the capacity for evil. This is evident in Christopher Browning's book entitled *Ordinary Men*. The book explores the path of the Reserve Police Battalion 101. These were middle-aged men from Hamburg who eventually became very instrumental in the mass execution of innocent Jews. Browning's main argument is that these men were ordinary individuals put into an unfortunate circumstance, and that they ultimately could have been anybody. He writes, "Within virtually every social collective, the peer group exerts tremendous pressures on behavior and sets moral norms." He then wraps up the novel by asking the question, what group cannot grow to be ordinary killers under such circumstances if these men could? It is scary and almost unrealistic for a sane mind to think about, but at the same time it appears to be the reality. For further proof, just take a look at either the Stanford Prison Experiment of 1971 or the Milgram Experiment of 1961.

The dark side of human nature is real. It can be scientifically accounted for, and environmentally provoked.

The dark side of human nature that I speak of doesn't always refer to evil acts against others, but also evil acts against you. The demons I speak of can easily manifest in fear, insecurity, addiction, lack of self-worth, anger, and numerous other emotional reactions that may not be considered necessarily evil by definition. When you choose fear instead of love, you are embracing the dark side. When you choose blame instead of inward assessment, you are embracing the dark side. When you choose self-hatred instead of acceptance, you are embracing the dark side. The key is to accept the dark side without letting it define you, and without remaining complacent in its reality.

I have many poems that explore this dark side of human nature. Some are more personal, while some are simply me stepping into the shoes of another individual and connecting with the emotions that might occupy the dark side of their soul. An example of the latter is a poem entitled "A Molester's Moleskin." This piece was inspired by Ted Bundy, Jeffery Dahmer, and other merciless serial killers who often raped their victims. Let me begin by stating that I have never personally had any serious urge to directly murder or forcefully fulfill my lustful urges without consent. That being said, I simply made a creative attempt to chronicle the mind of a molester. The piece entitled "Muted Devils" deals with the inability to confront the dark side of yourself, and instead simply "imagining figures of light" as Jung suggests in the opening quotation. The idea here isn't approval of the dark side, but rather acceptance. The devils in this piece don't refer to a figure that lives in fire and holds a pitchfork, but it rather refers to the devils inside of you. If you simply ignore these devils instead of confronting them, they could eventually lead to your demise. When you pretend as if they don't exist, you don't make them disappear, but you rather simply allow them to attack you unconsciously. Included in this section is one of my favorite pieces which is entitled "Goodbye...." This piece is a story about a female who appears perfect on the outside, but has issues deeper than the surface. Nobody can see past her outward appearance to actually care about the demons she is dealing with inside of her. The devils within her drive her insane and she eventually commits suicide and offers her deceased body to the individuals who desired it all along. This piece helps us explore the idea that everybody deals with their corrupt emotional responses, and the fact that nobody has immunity from the dark side. It also shows how putting people on illusory high pedestals often simply sets up a long inevitable fall.

Again, this section isn't a celebration of the demons, but simply an admittance and acceptance. In Christianity, it is the equivalent to confessing your sins to God. You can't be forgiven for unacknowledged sins, nor can you begin to clear your emotions without love for yourself and an acceptance of those unfavorable emotions.

My Journey Through Hell

I took a walk through Hell... just to see
Who I would find... and who was set free
I stepped inside those fiery pits
To see if it was real... see if it exists
There was no presence of a rapist... or a room for thieves
No place for conductors of murderous regimes
No home for the adulterer... terrorists were absent
No idol worshipers... nor lovers of fashion
No residence for the addict... the heroin fiend
Not even the dealer... or the man in-between
Blasphemous bastards never greeted my sight
As if Lucifer himself couldn't decipher wrong from right
But I walked... walked... peered into the darkness
How could the almighty Lord be so heartless?
I took a walk through Hell... and who did I see?
A priest... a doctor... a prophet... and me...

A Spirit's Confessional

Last night I killed a man... just to watch him bleed
He yelped and screamed as he fell to his knees
My knife met his flesh with the wrath of Hell
Such a cynical smile as I waved farewell
But the man was worthless... he embodied no purpose
Trouble inside made him suffer on the surface
Last night I killed a man... just to watch him die
I felt no remorse as my bullet pierced his eye
Maybe in the closet they won't find his corpse
I attempted to conceal him... but my efforts fell short
I set him ablaze to assure his death
I didn't sense regret... until he took his last breath
The almighty God forgives all who ask
But under circumstances... I can't complete that task
Last night I killed a man... just to watch him bleed
Only one problem... the man was me

Crazy

My mind has been a little off lately... or maybe it was never on
I feel like I'm dying... or maybe I was never born
Maybe I lived once and I already died
Maybe everything I've perceived has been a lie
Maybe I'm the devil... live in the flesh
Just to fill your mind with lust, greed, and stress
Maybe I'm an angel... following behind
Sent by the almighty on a destiny divine
I keep seeing flashes... I keep seeing lights
But yet it still seems I can't escape the night
I'm trapped in darkness where the unknown dwells
Trapped in darkness... just an unknown cell
They label me foolish... label me insane
I label them ignorant... not in tune with their brain
Flashes reappear... a white light is in the rear
Farewell... I think my time is near...

Muted Devils

Love for the light... despise for the darkness
Love for the compassionate... hate for the heartless
Crick in your neck from the abnormal one-sided views
Staring for infinite time at an angelic face
Selective vision... suppressed satanic prisons
Shooting Cupid's arrows with misdirected precision
Dionysus is left to flourish undetected
Like a cancerous cell internally mass murdering

Muted devils but the frequencies remain
Awakening the Lucifer depleted by the brain
Lingering in lustful Hedonism
Unaddressed and ignored by the virgin priest
Turtles while their shells lay blankets on their bones
Clipping off their wings turning human to stone
Staring for infinite time at an angelic face
While the muted devils stab and vanish without a trace

The Serpent

We all still abide in the garden today
The garden from which the first man was made
We all still ignore the divine instruction…
And we all still bite when we're under the seduction
No clothes to mask what appearance hides
But their bite uncovered the mask of the blind
On that fateful day… sin opened the gate
Some seem to think he left with no trace

The serpent has left his soul in the people
And with freewill… the sins are unequal
He instilled a desire to promote one's self
He looks unarmed… and moves in stealth
We are all evil… and have evolved into the creature
Who told lies… and wore the masquerade of a teacher
We have turned into the creature that turned against us
Jealous without love… we entice those who trust
Evading us is a must… you go away with the dusk
Until the sunrise reminds us the world is corrupt
Now nothing suffices… it's never good enough
Trapped in a world of greed and lust
Where living takes the soul… and leaves it in the dust
We are now the creature that once condemned us

Addicted

I'm addicted... addicted to the touch
Addicted... I can't get enough
Addicted... but the desire is lust
The man in the mirror is hard to trust
Every time we greet... I show disdain
But I can see his anguish... I can feel his pain
I love when the high takes over me
But I seem to never land where I'm supposed to be
When it's not in proximity... cold sweats erupt
I struggle to evade but my mind is corrupt
I struggle to evade but I can't get enough
Addicted... but the desire is lust
Society rebukes the very presence of my flesh
They say God will heal me... surely they jest
Maybe one day I can overcome this
Maybe if my efforts weren't so remiss

Troubled Waters

Cold world... dark clouds in the forecast
The downpours create troubled waters in the street
One troubled drop can turn virgin seas red...
And introduce Mary to the belly of the beast
In her belly is a beast...
Three triplets named Six intertwined at the feet
Stepping stones to that pedestal the blind seek

She thought Immaculate Conception...
But it was just a seed from the apple that Eve digested
The karma of her past manifesting in the present
Now a demon in disguise is manifesting in deception

Cold world... dark clouds in the forecast
The downpours create troubled waters in the street
Troubled waters in the oceans
Troubled waters in the seas
Troubled waters in my house...
Slowly rising to my knees

When it rains it pours,
But we're the ones to blame...
For not confronting the troubled waters,
The last time it rained

The waters don't disappear,
They rise to the skies...
Creating more dark clouds,
Our self-induced demise

Possessed

I love the darkness...
I love my mind's psychotic state
A disciple for the demons when tempted with the proper bait

I love the darkness...
I love my heart's quickened rhythm
A victim of the system trapped in my minds prison

I love the darkness...

I hate the suppression
I love the demons... But I hate the possession

A Molester's Moleskine

Father dead... absent patriarchal presence
Isolation... seclusion... now I'm forced into depression
Domesticated devils dismember my direction
And in drive the demons... now I'm forced into possession
The church calls me sinner... but I refuse to be "delivered"
Now this lavish of liquor always lingers in my liver
Psychedelic Sudafed... I see black holes of life
I'm doing disappearing acts with these white lines of death
Denied sex... so I put my victims in sedation
Hell on earth is the reality depicted in my basement
Abrasive... come dance in the devil's corridors
Await the fate of the decapitated whore

Depression

My mind whispers tales of contradiction
My body begs for sedatives and toxins
My heart yearns for the love I lack within
My soul is lonely...
It travels aimlessly through abstract realities
It guides me with an intangible map
My negligent ego denies the existence

Overridden with emotion
Insecurities intertwine with fear
Unaligned chakras and tattooed tears

Unsure of my direction
Waiting on depression
She intrudes into my residence
She kidnaps my joy and harasses my destiny
She hides my love and kills my gratitude
She worships my fear and pays tithes to toxins

When I feel I have nowhere to turn
Depression sets a fire within my heart...
And lets it burn

Goodbye…

I emerged from the heavens… that's what they say
My radiant eyes awake the day
Every woman's idol… every man's fantasy
Conceit invades me… I'm suffering from vanity
My beauty is immaculate… that's what they say
Eyes are drawn to my stunning display
What women dream to be… and what men dream of
With just one touch… they fall in love
If only they knew what lied beneath
Greed… lust… lies… deceit
If only they could see past the skin
And see the war that rages within
So the body you all want… the body you desire
Is now yours… as I feed my soul to the fire
Please don't mourn… please don't cry
Just take this body you longed for… and wave goodbye…

Tears

When did it all go wrong?
Such a quick conversion from dusk to dawn
The sun that glistened yesterday now blinds
Once high definition, now it can't be defined
The marvelous sound of company shifts to irritation
Your wild thrill is suddenly wished complacent
Maybe a lost love… maybe an unfulfilled search
Maybe it was death… maybe an unwanted birth
The voice of depression… the noise won't cease
Trying… but the only person you meet is defeat
Trying… but it's still in vain you seek
Trying… you knock… but the answer is bleak
The eyes are the window to a man's soul
So when it rains, the door of opportunity is closed
But when the rain stops… the sun shines bright
And the drops of your tears brought something to life

Love

"At the touch of love, everyone becomes a poet" –Plato

In my opinion, love is at the core of human existence. Love is the oneness that connects us to everything alive. Unconditional love is the state that most religions believe is at the core of the divine source, whether it be external or internal. Throughout history, numerous philosophers, artists, and entertainers have described how love has positively and negatively affected both their lives and people around them. I have decided to continue the tradition by offering my personal experiences, as well as my observations of the outside world concerning this four letter word. Growing up, I rarely ever heard love being spoken of with a negative connotation. My parents explained love in relation to marriage. They informed me that when two people love each other, they come together in holy union the way God intends us to. My parents also taught me love in relation to family, which began to show me how complex this one word could be. Between my parents and my Christian upbringing, I also learned about the love of God. I was told that no matter what I have done, if I humbly ask for forgiveness and repent, God will forgive me. The reason for this inevitable forgiveness was because of a thing called unconditional love.

It wasn't until I got older that I began to hear people speak of love as being able to do anything but provide comfort and security. In elementary school, I was intrigued and confused to discover that a friend of mine had parents that lived in two separate houses. When you grow up a certain way, you often create a bias within yourself and assume that everybody else experienced life's events in the way that you did. How could two people love each other, get married, have children, and then live in different households? This isn't the love that I was taught.

As I grew older, I began to see love depicted in the media, music, and movies in a negative, possessive, and insensitive light. At this stage in my life, I now understand where the confusion came from. I had grown up being informed about and shown unconditional love, while what I had begun to see throughout the media and entertainment industry was conditional and dependent love. Unfortunately, dependent love has often caused problems in our modern society. The laws of duality prohibit dependent love from being a purely positive experience. Duality tells us that without the opposite, the present state has no value. Light would have no value if it wasn't for the darkness. Money would have no value without the possibility of being broke. That being said, dependent love is only given power because of the conditions in which the opposing party is treating you. If the conditions changed to no longer benefit you, you would no longer love that person. That is dependent love, and that is where the possessiveness, control, and selfishness enter; because dependent love cannot coexist without dependent hate.

It is of my belief that true unconditional love is an exception to this rule. I believe that unconditional love is the oneness that ancient mystics have discussed throughout history, as well as the divine metaphysical experience of God. I don't believe human beings as a whole have evolved to the point where we are able to give non-stop unconditional love to everything alive and to our entire dualistic earthly experience. I believe we can make it possible, but it often times ends up being a localized and solitary effort. (i.e. a spouse or child) The emotion that I believe holds us back from experiencing unconditional love is fear. Because of this, my poetry is a reflection of the dependent love that is present upon this earth plane, as well as localized unconditional love. Maybe it is possible to completely transcend fear and give non-stop unconditional love to everybody and everything, but I have to speak only purely from the emotions that I have come in contact with and what I have visually seen through my personal experiences. Even if those experiences include future worries, past regrets, and channeling emotions from outside experiences I have witnessed either first hand or in the media, they all come from a true place. Even fictional creative stories that I scribe poetically are still deep-rooted in true emotional realities that I have just toyed with to artistically and imaginatively express.

One piece in this section is a poem entitled "How Can I Trust You?" In this piece I wrestle with the idea of trust, and come to the conclusion that trust is more internal than external. Often times we will develop a lack of trust for our significant other because of the fact that we are attempting to mask a lack of trust for ourselves. I don't believe that this dynamic only applies to trusting a mate, but rather it is existent in all forms of relationships and encounters. "Reunite" is simply a tale about lovers that have grown apart, and are wondering whether or not they were meant to be. It is basically a poetic expression of the old saying that if you love it you should let it go. If you let it go, and destiny finds a way to bring you back together, then you can be certain that it was meant to be. In "Love is a Bully", I depict love in the negative light that is often a result of dependent love. The once positive experience is now responsible for you feeling regret, shame, and heartbreak. "Words to My Wife" is a creative personal exploration of the type of love that I would hope to receive and give to my wife from the future. It concludes by saying that the love we endure together will never die, even in the unfortunate event that my body were to perish from this earth before hers. It seems that in hoping for love that never dies, I am searching for this unconditional love that coincides with my upbringing and keeps me morally grounded in my beliefs.

Mathematics

One soul... one heart... one spirit... one mind
Two eyes to lead the way... so he shall seek and find
Two feet to walk the path... two legs to guide
One soul... one spirit... contacting the divine
One brain to learn what they won't teach him in classes
One mouth to recite his life journey to the masses
One nose to smell deception... one God for protection
And only one choice... for the thousand directions
Two arms to support his two helping hands
Two ears to listen... maybe soon he'll understand
He turns to his heart... when things get rough
The only thing he has... when the math doesn't add up

How Can I Trust You?

How can I trust you?
I don't trust myself

I know my good deeds could easily be infiltrated with corrupt
thoughts
I know my evil lies dormant...
Awaiting the proper environment to prosper
Ready to contradict what I stand for
Ready to break vows and destroy empathy

Should I deceive myself?
Deceive myself into immunity from the forces of darkness?
It might even last long enough to title my eulogy
But it would only be a concealment of facts never challenged by the
lawyer

How can I trust you?
I don't trust myself

Distant Lover

The months pass by... and so do the years
The rain comes down... and so do the tears
The trees keep growing... and so does my heart
The sun rises up... but I'm left in the dark
Your glistening eyes resemble the stars
But it seems that your love is just that far
Behind the window I glance... I've seen better days
My angel is somewhere amidst the haze
Her love is like the horizon... she remains at a glance
One day I'll take her hand... one day we shall dance
I love you so.... yet you seem so far
I love you so... but don't know who you are
The months pass by... and so do the years
The rain comes down... and so do the tears
The trees keep growing... and so does my heart
I watch the sunrise... but still... I'm left in the dark

Reunite

It's easy to think that my heart turned cold
As I peer into the future… and can't see it unfold
A journey toward love was the path foretold
But I feel it's being ripped… by a force I can't control
It's easy to believe that I lost all hope
But I just lost patience… in my desire to devote
In a desire to take my pride and digest
It's held back by my vanity… a burden on my chest
I can't pinpoint the moment the progression ceased
When the cold winds of the west started drifting to the east
When you lose so many relationships
You feel like you just can't relate or commit
It's easy to believe I want to let you go
Because what I feel… my conceit won't let me show
So I'll let you go… and watch you march through the night
Hoping destiny finds us… and we reunite

Betrayal of Sanity

I loved her touch… I never let go
She helped me sustain… helped me grow
Gave me sight… amidst the dark
I felt we could never… ever grow apart
She hid my subconscious… from the eyes of the masses
But her resistance to my love was oh so passive
She slowly… slowly… drifted away
But it occurred too subtle to reassure her stay
Something has come over me… since the day she left
I'm somebody else… I have no identity left
One day I'm blissful… the next day I'm depressed
One day I'm at ease… the next day I'm stressed
This man in the mirror is beginning to haunt me
A lost and coldhearted man is what I see
I need to restore her everlasting love
Maybe I'll forget… if I soak my brain in blood

Love is a Bully

Love is a bully
She feeds on weak susceptible souls
She lacks operating optics so she kills at random
Infesting minds and silencing the voices of intellect
Triggering unforeseen patience
Robbing her victims of green faces

Love is a bully
Mercy is crossed out in her dictionary
Bringing emotions to the surface that lied dormant for years
The faceless villain invades your face with tears
Many have attempted to convict her of her crimes
She seems to only grow deadlier with time

One problem…
Love is a bully you can't report to an authority
She has no physical identity
And you can't warn future victims of her venomous hand
If they've never been attacked then they wouldn't understand

Words to My Wife

At this stage in my life… I don't know who you are
But something tells me you may not be too far
I refuse to rush… I fell in love with patience
But when our paths do cross… our bond I'll hold sacred
I hope that my pride doesn't destroy our peace
I hope that our love will only increase
I hope that lust won't corrupt my soul
For it is with you…. that I am made whole
Never will I deceive… and never will I lie
I pledge to remain faithful… until the day I die
And to my unborn child… we will one day conceive
Together we will insure the world doesn't mislead
On that fateful day… in the event of my demise
I hope my ears don't allow me to hear your cries
But on that fateful day… as you wave goodbye
Before the casket shuts… just look into my eyes
And know that if you need me… just look into the sky
Because the love we have… will never ever die

More Than a Rose

The cliché gift for the one you love
Used to accompany the lonely dove
Hoping this gift will yield me the key
But what we have is deeper than the eye can see
Deeper than any gift of elegant taste
Deeper than our past we have yet to erase
Deeper than a touch… deeper than a kiss
Deeper than the sea… and its beautiful bliss
More than a possession… more than a ring
More than any note in a song I could sing
More than a glance… more than lust
More than the world… you're more than enough
More than these words that I scribe to you
In hopes that one day they'll come alive to you
What I'm giving you is more than a rose
What I'm giving you is a promise… that you'll never be alone

All That Matters

In a place where those deceive and lie
The place that provides what you desire with your eyes
But never acknowledges what you desire with your heart
Predestined to fail... doomed from the start
In a place where those are reluctant to lead
And pass the trait down to their unborn seed
The present is predicted by the past's mistakes
And shows all possibility that the past creates
In a place where temptation reigns supreme
And resentfulness is silent... we join the team
In a world where deception wears a velvet glove
In the midst of the world... all we need is love

Glimmers of Hope

"We must be the change we wish to see in the world" -Mahatma Gandhi

Being exposed to things such as global warfare, inhumane corporate agendas, alleged mind control, and force-fed religious doctrine led me to begin losing hope in the human race. However, after all of the self-reflecting and the acceptance of my own insecurities, I began to regain my faith and positive outlook. Again, inward work is the recurring theme that began to rear its beautiful physique. Inward work was what led to my eventual glimmers of hope and optimism about life. It began with having a better grasp on optimism and hope within my own life, as opposed to casting judgment on the world and believing that everybody had a self-centered ulterior motive.

A work of literature that had a profound impact on my life outlook was *The Celestine Prophecy* by James Redfield. This book is a fictional spiritual journey told in first person. It gives readers the sense that they are taking the journey directly for themselves as each chapter gradually reveals spiritual insights. What made the book so influential for me was the fact these spiritual insights seemed to uncover inherent beliefs that I had felt but had never been able to articulate and communicate verbally. It also brought me back into my conscious perspective of destiny through intuitive guidance and synchronicity. Coincidentally, these were the same principles I had been taught throughout my upbringing. In church, this intuitive guidance and synchronicity would be referred to as the guidance of the Holy Spirit and attuning to the will of God. My life began to have more inner clarity, and I began to attempt being the change I wanted to see throughout the world instead of believing that the outward world was the solitary thing that needed change. I was also able to look at the bigger picture of how our collective unconscious has grown and evolved throughout all of our years of inhabiting this earth. This realization gave me the hope for humanity that I had once guarded myself from with my own self-doubt.

Around this time I also began to explore the importance of a life with balance. I've come to the conclusion that everything in your life must be appropriately balanced in a quest for unconditional happiness and a decrease of dependency. For me, this began with attempting to take spirituality and oneness, and cohesively blend them with the personality and the ego. I believe spirituality reigns supreme over all of the dealings on this limited three dimensional earth plane. This belief became troublesome only when I used that fact to deem earthly dealings as having no importance or relevance. Coincidentally, I began to lose touch with my personality and ego, simply deeming them as illusions that were holding me back from the limitless potential of spiritual experiences. However, I began to see that this state of mind was troublesome, simply because of the fact that I was beginning to ignore the realities of this earth plane in which I have been placed. Ignoring these realities created a lack of balance, as well as a state of denial. Consciously accepting and trying to seek balance in all the experiences of life has proven to be most beneficial to me. In Buddhism, this principle is referred to as the middle way. Early in his life, the Buddha attempted to follow a strictly spiritual and self-mortifying path. This path eventually led to him starving himself, and attempting to rid himself of all earthly desires. After almost killing himself due to starvation, this experience led him towards his discovery of the middle way. The middle way is the common ground between sensual indulgence and self-mortification. This is what the Buddha called enlightenment. For me, ignoring the ego and pretending as if it was non-existent simply led to the mirror effect. I began to see the ego reflected in everybody else and began to despise it. Once again, I didn't realize I was simply despising something within myself. More self-reflection was needed.

In my poem "A Love Story", I intricately describe complex love dealings between the past, present, future, life, and death. I included this particular piece in this section because I believe it accurately represents the optimism I gained through acceptance and balance. "Beautiful" is one of my favorite pieces. Everybody has heard the clichés about everybody being beautiful in their own way, but one day I was struck with a revelation that seemed to resonate with me deeper than the clichés ever did. I began to see beauty in a new light. Instead of attempting to describe it in a structural sentence, I'll let you read poetically the mind-state that I had begun to develop. The piece, "Dear Ego" is something that I wrote during my period of ego rejection and suppression, when I believed that the ego and personality were less important than oneness and spirituality. Now I believe in the interdependent balance between the two worlds that combine together to represent the full human experience.

A Love Story

I've loved her... ever since adolescence
She's always been with me... her name is PRESENT
She's always so faithful... but I'm never satisfied
The looks of her friend always catch my eye
Her friend's name is FUTURE... but she never seems to receive me
I can never even touch her... all she does is tease me
The longer I stare... her appearance declines
Maybe it's because I left PRESENT behind
Sometimes my ex-girlfriend tries to resurface
Her name is PAST... she blinds me of my purpose
Me and her are really close... she's far from a stranger
But she has faults... and she won't let me change her
When it comes to PAST... I've lost all respect
Ever since she wanted us to ménage with DEATH
So I decided to marry PRESENT... and make her my wife
After we made love... we gave birth to LIFE

Beautiful

Through the eyes of the divine... every face is perfection
But we alter God's trace... just to chase a perception
So we model after the models... the look that's accepted
Made in God's image... but that look is rejected
But I don't think a child sees through those same eyes
With an urge to conform to that same disguise
But when they're individuals... they're cast away like lepers
So they begin to conform to that same design
They begin to hold back their emotions... so timid... out of fear
Thinking what's beautiful to them... isn't beautiful to their peers
Over their shoulder they peer... their opinion is diminished
Love is left out... because love is blind to an image
An image of "beautiful" is imbedded in our minds
An image that needs to be left behind
Once we see beauty from divine optics
We'll see beauty in everything the divine hands made
And those beautiful eyes... from which the divine watches...
Sees hatred on His creations... and He feels betrayed
Beauty isn't measured by the size of one's lips...
The curves of one's hips... or the color of their hair
We're not searching for beauty... we're searching for an image
Because beauty was always there...
We're just too consumed with an image of perfection to admit it
Or to even realize it's there...
But honestly... I don't think we even care

Dear Ego

Up until now... I was bewildered in confusion
Separating our connection, but we are all the same
Dear ego... you are simply an illusion
An illusion that it seems we cannot contain

Hatred... envy... no sympathy is shown
Just greed... lust... ignorance is sown
Power is misused... obtained for control
Materials are abused... silencing the soul

War has erupted... where the innocent dwell
War against humanity... war against ourselves
Justifying our attack with good cause... or religion
Our cause is unity... but the effect is division

Farewell ego... our time is done
I now realize everything on this earth is one
A shift in our consciousness... has now begun
Let's let go of our egos... and see what we can become

The Middle Way

Same path… infinite perspectives
Infinite moral judgments to apply in vain
The gift and curse of the brain

Recognizing prideful personality
Detaching from it to experience oneness
Finding the middle way
Transcending the one-sided view of dualistic nature

Same picture… infinite words
Infinite connections
Infinite emotions driven by the past and present

Recognizing labels and comparisons
Detaching from it to experience oneness
Finding the middle way
Transcending past worries and future hopes
Living in the moment

As We Evolve

The world spins trapped in a cosmos of stars
On the surface we watch the sun set from afar
Entering a dark period... that ends with the day
When the illumination of the sun makes the moon fade away
First formed were the skies... the firmament... the heavens
One land mass was separated into seven
The waters of life would soon flow with grace
Then God created man... in the likeness of his face
We swim through the depths of the rivers of the womb
Soon to rest in the depths of the soil... below our tomb
There must be more... to this intricate design
Than just watching the sunrise... and the stars align
We must observe the caves in which we used to survive
As it transitioned to this technological place we reside
Envisioning the steps of how we came to be
We can evolve past this physical shell we see
Emerging from the flesh... we are one with the divine
Emerging to the spirit... which can stand the test of time

The Unlikely Future

Collective consciousness... eradicated egos
Humanitarian habitants... lasting love lingers
Greed is at the graveyard... covered in blood
Murdered by empathy and smothered with love

Behind the Curtain

Political prophets preaching to the sheep
Making political profits privately and discrete
Deception from all directions lacking discretion
Sly salvation... supporting suppression
They empathize to avoid enemies
Nihilistic negotiating with powerful pleas
The crowd on their knees... pledging to a flag
Digesting decrees from people with degrees

But behind the curtain... and behind the emotionless face
There's an empathetic human that's hard to erase
Maybe hard to trace... but it dwells beyond the fame
It cries behind the lies... in the right side of the brain

Oneness and the connection to everything alive...
Lies behind the curtain unveiled when we die

Survive

Basking in the glory of this complex creation
Yet we're complacent... stagnant in the scenery
Cutting down the greenery... to construct paper for me to scribe
this
Watching businesses exploit egos and denied gifts

Perplexed personas... hypocritical judgments
Egotism rains on an ice cold brain
Skating in circles on a frozen terrain
Any second the thin ice will submerge us
We'll be floating in a cold stream with the excess waste
Corporation corpses signal elitisms demise
The masquerades decay... the eulogy of the disguise
Drowning in the tears that the rebel cries

Let the tsunami waves hide the graves
And crucify the religions that designed the slaves
Then we can awaken to the potentials we're denied
Actually avoid the revelations and survive

As the River Flows

"It is not the strongest of the species that survives, nor the most intelligent that survives. It is the one that is the most adaptable to change." –Charles Darwin

In my opinion, naturally running water in a stream, river, creek, or ocean is one of the most beautiful, peaceful, and serene sounds known to man. In addition, I believe that the way in which it transforms, adapts, and continually flows is one of the most beautiful and inspirational sights known to man. To me, the sound always brings me back to the natural flow of the universe. A Taoist would describe it as embracing yourself in "the Tao", or "the way." Nature is a wonderful indication and representation of the process of decay and renewal. It is a glorious representation of the endless life cycle.

Often times, I believe that we are so hung up on past regrets and future worries that we forget about the eternal present state. The eternal present state of existence is all that there is. The past and future are simply illusions. Observing nature also made me conclude that we ourselves are a part of nature. The sound of the wind puts me in tune with the universe and the present moment, but so does my breathing when I pay attention to it. The sounds of birds and crickets remind me of the natural and unpredictable rhythm of the universe, but so does a crowd of people that are all immersed in conversation. People always discuss re-enchanting with nature, but in my opinion I don't believe that there was anything to re-enchant with in the first place. It is already embodied within us once we are open to the experience.

Chuang Tzu once said that "The perfect man employs his mind as a mirror; it grasps nothing; it refuses nothing; it receives, but does not keep." I believe that this statement embodies the sense of detachment that many eastern religions believe is the path to enlightenment. There is a Buddhist principle that provided me with a way to experience this detachment while sill embracing everything within the present moment. To paraphrase, this principle stated that because nothing is permanent, we should view everything as already dead. In essence, we should view every plant as already withered, and we should view every glass as already broken. In my opinion, when you maintain this viewpoint, every moment becomes precious, distinct, and irreplaceable. This places you within the parameters of the eternal flow of the universe. To me, being in the flow of the universe also means accepting those things that are inconceivable to us. While we accept these things, this should still not deter us from asking questions, constructing theories, and creating experiments to test these theories.

The poem entitled "Mother Nature" basically describes my viewpoint that we are one with nature. It describes nature as projections of our own feelings and emotions within. In the end, what is it that really makes us so different from the rest of nature? The piece entitled "Embrace" discusses the concept of duality throughout nature. It argues that maintaining your sanity through this complex world of ups and downs comes when you embrace the good and bad as one whole exuberating experience. It also refers to the acceptance of the positive and negative parts that dwell inside of you. "Decay and Renewal" is a poem I wrote while sitting in nature, and recognizing the similarities through all of the living things. Everything lacked permanence, and everything had the ability to create.

When you're a child, you are curious about everything. Nature is beautiful, and you ponder the existence of all of the different life forms including your own. You see the world and the entire universe as a giant playground that you can explore. Many of us lose this sense of wonder as we grow older. I believe that the key to getting back in tune with the miracle of nature and the universe is by getting back in touch with our inner child. I also believe that this adds limitless creative and exploratory potential. Pablo Picasso once said that "Every child is an artist. The problem is staying an artist when you grow up." A potential hypothesis could be that the child is more connected and attuned to the flow of the universe.

The theme of this whole book is the acceptance of all that you are in this present moment and embracing it regardless of what society's perceptions of good and bad are. While I have personally not reached a state of unconditional happiness, I believe that the key lies in acceptance. Nature is the perfect metaphor for this acceptance. The leaves don't fight against the wind, and the river does not fight against the current. This doesn't afford you the permission to be irresponsibly complacent, but simply the ability to attune to the will of Godly love. It affords you the permission to become the river that flows with the current, and to become the mountain that stands firm in the face of adversity.

I would also like to add that even though I have seemed to find peace and acceptance with many parts of myself, I have not completely transcended all of these phases that are discussed throughout the book. For instance, I still have battles in my head concerning religious beliefs and I still have fear of being controlled by outside forces. Proposing solutions to these issues doesn't turn me into a robot that can automatically apply these principles without any sort of resistance from the parts of me that I am attempting to transcend. As long as these emotions continue to exist on this three dimensional plane, I will continue to scribe them poetically. This is simply the full human experience. These are all parts of me and my perceptions that represent my poetic truth.

As the River Flows

As the river flows… life goes on
In the midst of the rain that falls from the storm
Sometimes it flows swift… at times it is slow
The creatures of the sea still exist below
At no point have I seen its movement cease
As it pours its soul into the belly of the beast
At no point have I seen it run dry
It was here before life… so it will never die
It helps sustain life… without it none exists
For that reason… it's surrounded by a world of bliss
As the river flows… I can see tomorrow
It camouflages my tears… masks my sorrow
So I say to the river… please take me away
Where no one is there to cast stones or betray
As the river flows… suffering is foregone
As the river flows… life goes on

Following the Rain Drops

Gazing out the window... I've seen better days
The drops of April's tears have replaced the sun's rays
She cries with such passion... cries with such pain
The good times have departed... bliss has been slain
But the drops of her tears bring flowers to life
The necessary evil... the possum's plight
Depression invades us... subdued by the force
Following the drops... as I survey the source
Following the drops down sidewalks and streets
They fall on my tongue... I can taste defeat
Following the drops through the rivers and creeks
It rises to my knees... but I can't retreat
I cry rivers of sorrow... rivers of grief
Yet in the distance... I saw hope and relief
I thought this rain would confine me... make me lose control
Until I saw an ocean... that could swallow it whole

Sages of the Sea

Soliciting the sages of the sea
Poseidon's infinite disciples
Immersed in the acceptance unseen by politicians
Submerged in the moment exclusive to the youth
Balanced with internal darkness ignored by the priest
Balanced with internal light forgotten by the fearful
Murderers... Drowning the corpses of the veils
All seven are greeted by the floors of the ocean
Fear, anger, and greed...
Accompanied by laziness and desire
Topped with the mask of pride and conditional love
The veils overused by the manipulative ego

The sages of the sea... grounded in the seasons
Offering insight to loud minds and fearful hearts
Simplifying the stressors architected by the brain
Basking in the sun... and flowing with the rain

Sounds of Nature

The sounds of nature make me whole
Its innocence is like that of a child
It steadily beats to the rhythm of my soul
There are no speakers in the wild

Its innocence is like that of a child
The free flowing compositions caress my ears
There are no speakers in the wild
Hopes for tomorrow suppress my fears

The free flowing compositions caress my ears
It steadily beats to the rhythm of my soul
Hopes for tomorrow suppress my fears
The sounds of nature make me whole

Mother Nature

Infinite bliss... letting go of fear
Mother Nature's breath levitates my consciousness
She cries tears of joy...

Tears of joy to quench the thirst of her greenery
Nourishing the souls that inhabit her abode

Mother Nature...
Is she just a metaphor for the beauty within?
A way for us to dissect our bodies?
Imaginatively displacing our inner beauty onto our projection of the
world?

Infinite sorrow... one with fear
Mother Nature's wind stifles commute
She cries tears of pain...

Tears of pain to drown
Flooding the streets we built to neglect her

Mother Nature...
Is she just a metaphor for the discomfort within?
A way for us to dissect our bodies?
Imaginatively displacing our inner fears onto our projection of the
world?

Maybe we ARE Mother Nature...
Without separation...
One with creation.

Embrace

This seesaw of life is weighed down with closed boxes
Yin with no yang... these are verses full of vices
Imbalanced chemicals creating lines at the asylum
Ironically they also breed full cathedrals
The addict snorts away the thin lines that divide us
And offer scapegoats the stone-throwers can hit
Sympathy silenced when their lines lead to caskets
While the tearless search for a street called straight in Damascus

This seesaw of life is weighed down with a gavel
Covering skeleton bones hiding in the gravel
Bones that are growing into cannibals
Eating you alive in a jealous rage
A savage created by a false sanity
Yang with no yin... these are verses full of vices
The sane is a gracious moon... a heartless sun
Embracing his light and his darkness as one

Everything Was One

Everything was one
Before everything begun
I was you
You were me
Everything was how it was supposed to be

We have fooled ourselves...
Fooled ourselves into thinking outside forces control us
Thinking they close doors to ultimate perception
Thinking they paint shut the windows of hope
Denied freedom cries force us into blame

Everything is one
The stars, the moon, the sun
I am you
You are me
Everything is how it's supposed to be

Decay and Renewal

Decay and renewal…
Watching the water flow with life
Collecting dead tree branches
Branches transformed into a damn by the beaver
To sustain their own life that the tree now lacks

Decay and renewal…
Lightning bugs embodying life
Lightning bolts striking it down
Birds chirp for impermanent mates
Reproducing impermanent seeds awaiting their same fate

Decay and renewal…
The stars we shoot for will one day cease to shine
The star that gives us life won't forever caress the hills of the east in
the early dawn
It is the flow of nature…
An eternal decay and renewal

Seasons

The season of fall… the autumn breeze
The degrees fall… and so do the leaves
The sun sheds light on radiant impermanent colors
Colors placed in body bags after falling to their death
Leaving a tree of life that stands bare
Producing artwork to accompany despair
The blanket of snow is a gift and a curse
Sometimes it graces… other times it erases
The grass on the other side is no longer appealing
The blades lie dormant for the snowflake concealing
Snowflakes to soon melt and rise to the skies
Falling and sprouting leaves as April cries
Falling and aiding the grass as it grows
The same grass it harasses when it snows
What is the reason?
In humans we call it bipolar
In nature we call it seasons

Bonus Poetry

There are a few additional poems that I wished to include in this collection. The only problem arose when I couldn't figure out how to categorize them to cohesively blend them with the previous sections. Rather than placing them inside random sections where they don't fit and throw off the flow of the book, I decided to give them their own section. Enjoy.

Social Networks

Stop it...
You keep detaching me from my reality
Feeding the mouth of my resistance
Entertaining my sheepskin covered with this pigmented flesh
Boredom sends you invitations unconsciously
Making time advance at record speeds
Procrastination loves you
My problems are momentarily sentenced to death
But they always survive...

Alternate worlds and infinite falsifications
All in search of gratification
I need to resist this temptation

Social networks...
Connected to everybody else
Disconnected from myself

The Woman

The digester of the apple... the reason why we sin
The bearer of temptation... she enters within
The sly fox that deceives us... seducer of our hearts
A false sense of protection... they proceed to depart

The shoulder for our head... the comforter indeed
Her tears are real... her heart is on her sleeve
The power to stand strong... the power to believe
The generator of faith... that sprouts from the seed

The weak piece of matter we were made to seduce
The victim of the pain... center of the abuse
We lay down with her... we depart at the end
Breaking her heart... where it cannot mend

The bearer of our children... the giver of life
Beauty under the sun... consoling at night
The ever present being in our lifelong pursuit
On whom we can depend... the woman... our roots

Chemical Imbalance

Sanity silenced... if it ever even spoke
It's hard to speak when rope strangles my throat
Hanging, letting suffocation sacrifice my spirit
Premeditated pain to permanently paralyze
Closing these constantly corrupted pair of eyes
Deafening ears prone to deception and misdirection
Shutting this mouth that emulates authority
Digesting their *will to power* diminishing what is orderly
Master-moral code capsizing enslaved sheep
Nihilism, denied visions... while evading the meek
Constraining the weak... prosperous positions
Constructing competition to entertain the sheep
God is dead... not the true divine presence
But the invented superstition made in man's image
Created to head this patriarchal pandemic
That comes alive in the lies wearing ties in the senate
Ancient math leads to the demise of the limit
Cracked atoms in the blackness to collide with the finish
Sanity silenced... now my mind speaks fluent
The free thought and potential that's denied to the student

Sea of Contrast

Differing opinions don't have to conflict
Similar waves topple dissimilar fish
Similar waves misguiding dissimilar ships
Similar stars... for everybody's dissimilar wish
Culture and ideals... blinded by the bias
Clinging to traditions giving reason to divide us
Philosophy and religion... nobody agrees
So everybody conforms to what nobody believes
Give a conflicting opinion... and they wanna debate you
Building relationships you can't even relate to
Open minds seem to appease the soul
Living in this sea of contrast is our solitary goal
Imagine if the whole world was the same
Same race... same religion... even the same names
There'd be no reason to live... nothing to attain
We'd be living in vain

Spiritual Slaughter

Behind the mask of misdirection and culture
The loving soul is turned wicked by the vultures
The soul of serenity subdued by satans
Dwellers of this hazardous hell... harboring hatred
Unaligned with the source we collide with a corpse
Spiritually deceased, we let his egotism preach
We let the mouths of dead men infiltrate our own speech
Until we too lay deceased...

Spiritual Evolution

Prophecy predictions… preposterous propositions
Righteous revelations recognized in the religions
A big bang reversed… the demise of the collision
Or spiritual awakening that's blinded by tradition
Tradition… that led to reformation demonstrations
Diminishing materials so the spirit could awaken
Creation… science… authoritative defiance
Violence… conflicting ideologies to blind us
Force-fed fiction… devil disguised diction
Friction… corrupt soothsayer superstition
Until spiritual evolutions, there's no need for revolutions
Prestigious persecution replaced by poor pollution

Memoirs of a King

I used to envy the people they praise
From envy... to spite
From spite to rage

I wanted them to love me
I wanted their love to run deeper... and deeper
And it did...
But only before they cut me... deeper... and deeper

I wanted them to kiss me
I wanted them to kiss me long in the morning and the night
And they did...
Only before their guns gave me a long kiss goodnight

I got what I wanted
They praised me as I wished
And I thought it would end with happiness and bliss

The throne was much different... from what I once thought
A lot of kings lose their head
And as for the rest...
Their head gets cut off

Nameless

I wish I was born without a title
Why is identification so vital?
Bearing the name of the ones who bore me
Expected to become who existed before me
Now when I walk they expect to see...
Somebody else standing next to me
Somebody who validates who I will become
Their path is mine... the feeling is numb
I'm anti-traditions... rather I'm ambitious
Don't categorize me on account of my conditions
I wish I was born without a face
Someone former is who they embrace
Someone who is similar in class and race
Please don't let them decide my fate
I wish I was born without an identity
So that when I die... people will remember ME
Not who you thought I would be...

Wisdom

Innocence… ignorance… naïve by decision
Should the blissful soul be wary of wisdom?
Does the all-knowing sage have peace of mind?
Or is he constantly at war with every piece of his mind?
Grappling with concepts nonexistent to the ignorant
Adding stressors to a brain that loves to bask in innocence
Does wisdom add responsibility without ability?
Or does it add divinity and help you see vividly?

The ignorant is like an infant…
Stagnant in a primal philosophical phase
Married to complacency…
Dodging rice grains as their foot steps over the broom
While their peers plant flags, leaving footsteps on the moon

The ignorant is selfish…
Denying the oneness and collective unconscious
Denying the evolution proposed by the prophets
Using past lifetimes as a crutch
Leaving future lifetimes in the dust

Wisdom is selfless…
Growing in the midst of inevitable death

But the wise dies like a star…
Letting her dust evolve in the midst of her demise
Letting off energy and lighting up the sky

Epilogue

"Good men must die, but death cannot kill their names" -Unknown

There is one more reason that I chose to publish this book of my poetry that I did not mention in the introduction. The final reason that I write this book is because I will one day die, just like everybody else. However, people who have made their mark through great strides in the history of human existence have developed a bit of immortality. Gandhi is dead. Mother Teresa is dead. Martin Luther King Jr. is dead. The list goes on. While these individuals have physical bodies that have perished into the dust from which they came, their ideas and ideologies still continue to stand the test of time. Their lives still have modern day significance. If Jesus Christ would have kept all of his revelations and ways of understanding the world to himself, we would not have Christianity as we know it and the whole dynamic of western religion would have been shifted. These statements aren't my ego attempting to assure itself prominence and power until the end of time, but rather they are a wake-up call to the entire world. Everybody has a story, and everybody's story deserves to be told. This is just my way of telling mine. None of us can afford to do humanity the disservice of withholding our viewpoints and individual truths. This is how our society continues to evolve. Everybody dies… why not die for the truth. Why not die for YOUR truth.

The Path to Immortality

Death is a tunnel… we all must navigate
Though inevitable… we long to stay awake
When running from the tomb… there's no way to escape
The morgue is a conviction… confirmed by fate
Death is but a portal… to everlasting life
Free of pain… desolation… and strife
But if you leave nothing to develop your seeds
You too are mortal… departing with the leaves
Who has contacted immortal terrain?
Perhaps those names we don't speak in vain
Who has opened the door to perpetual life?
Perhaps the man who's works we recite
If my words are not subdued by the hands of time
Perhaps through them… I can remain alive
One day… before my spirit and soul sever
I will attain the unfeasible… and live forever

"If my poetry aims to do anything, it's to deliver people from the limited ways in which they see and feel"

-Jim Morrison